Copyright ©2002 Els Feteris-Stam

All Rights Reserved. Published in the United States of America.
Printed in China.

Chitra Publications
2 Public Avenue
Montrose, Pennsylvania 18801-1220

No part of this publication may be reproduced or transmitted in any form
or by any means, electronic or mechanical, including photocopy, recording,
or any information storage and retrieval system now known or to be invented,
without permission in writing from the publisher, except by a reviewer
who wishes to quote brief passages in connection with a review
written for inclusion in a magazine, newspaper, or broadcast.

First Printing: 2002

Library of Congress Cataloging-in-Publication Data

Feteris-Stam, Els, DATE
   It's a small world : mini quilts from the Netherlands : 13 creative designs / by Els Feteris-Stam.
      p. cm.
   ISBN 1-885588-44-5 (pbk.)
    1. Quilting--Patterns. 2. Patchwork--Patterns. 3. Miniature quilts--Netherlands. I. Title.

TT835 .F48 2002
746.46'041--dc21

2002018805

Edited by: Debra Feece and Joyce Libal
Design and Illustrations: Diane M. Albeck-Grick
Photography: Van Zandbergen Photography, Brackney, Pennsylvania,
Stephen J. Appel Photography, Vestal, New York,
and Guy Cali Associates, Inc., Clarks Summit, Pennsylvania

Our Mission Statement:

*We publish quality quilting magazines and books
that recognize, promote, and inspire self-expression.
We are dedicated to serving our customers
with respect, kindness, and efficiency.*

www.QuiltTownUSA.com

Introduction

Making miniature quilts is a great passion of mine. Most of my quilts are my original designs, but occasionally I translate a design or method that I've seen in a large quilt into a smaller version of my own. Sometimes I enjoy the challenge of making a quilt as small as possible. That was the case with "Baskets (Mandjes)" on page 20.

The smaller the pieces of fabric used in a miniature quilt are, the bigger the contrast between the fabrics must be. Now and then I stitch a little block that ends up in the dustbin because its fabrics just did not contrast with each other properly. So I start making that little block all over again. I don't mind because it's a learning process that I enjoy very much. I've made more than a hundred quilts since taking up the craft about 13 years ago.

I'm very proud that, after writing a few patchwork books in Dutch, this book is being published in English in the United States. I originally designed most of these quilts for a workshop I give called "Every Month a Mini Quilt." The students who attend this workshop make the quilts in their own choice of fabrics. It's always surprising to see the finished quilts. Although everybody uses the same pattern, the outcome is always unique.

A few of the little quilts included here were made as entries for the Miniatures from the Heart Contest held annually by *Miniature Quilts* magazine. This contest provides me with a lot of inspiration and, to my surprise, I have even won a few times. When entering each contest I aspire to the limits of miniature quilt making, often experimenting with new methods or using the smallest fabric pieces possible. After each contest I assimilate what I have learned into lessons for my students.

It seems like I'm constantly occupied with quilting, sewing, and dreaming about possible new fabrics and quilt designs. If you want to see my latest work, you can always visit my website at www.bobbin.nl.

I think you will enjoy making the quilts presented here. I wish you much FUN with each and every stitch!

Els Fekerio-Stan

Contents

Mine Home Is Where Mine Heart Is (Mijn Huis Is Waar Mijn Hart Is)	4
My Dutch Neighborhood (Mijn Hollands Buurtje)	6
Indian Wedding Ring	8
Pots and Plants (Potten en Planten)	10
Plaids (Ruitjes)	12
Lily (Lelie)	14
Black Spider (Zwarte Spin)	16
Happy Spools (Vrolijke Klossen)	18
Baskets (Mandjes)	20
Hearts of Nine (Harten Negen)	22
Sunflowers (Zonnebloemen)	24
The Wheel of Adventure (Rad van Avontuur)	26
Mystery Stars (Mysterie Sterren)	28
General Directions	31

Mine Home Is Where Mine Heart Is

Fusible appliqué and foundation piecing meet in this folk-art neighborhood.

Mijn Huis Is Waar Mijn Hart Is

MATERIALS
- Assorted medium and dark print and plaid scraps, each at least 3" square
- 9 beige plaid scraps, each at least 4 1/2" x 5 1/2"
- 1/8 yard light print for the house blocks
- Black scraps, each at least 1 3/4" x 2", for the doors
- Black print, at least 2 1/2" x 12", for the cornerstones
- 1/2 yard black stripe for the stems, middle border, and binding
- Fat eighth (11" x 18") green plaid
- 3/8 yard dark green floral
- 22" x 26" piece of backing fabric
- 22" x 26" piece of thin batting
- Paper for the foundations
- Fusible web
- 8 assorted buttons
- 1 heart-shaped button
- Black and brown embroidery floss

QUILT SIZE: 19 1/4" x 24"
BLOCK SIZE: 3 3/4" x 4 7/8"

CUTTING
Pattern pieces (pages 29 and 30) for fusible appliqué are full size and do not need a turn-under allowance. Trace each pattern on the paper side of the fusible web. Rough cut around the traced shapes. Following the manufacturer's directions, fuse the shapes to the wrong side of appropriate fabric scraps. Cut them out on the drawn lines. All other dimensions include a 1/4" seam allowance. Fabric for foundation piecing will be cut as you stitch the blocks. Each piece must be at least 1/2" larger on all sides than the section it will cover. Refer to the General Directions, *as needed*. NOTE: *The blocks are numbered 1 through 9, starting in the top left corner and working left to right in each row. The pattern pieces for each block are labeled with that block number. Stitch the pieces for each block in alphabetical order.*

For each of 9 appliqué blocks:
- Cut one of each pattern piece unless otherwise indicated on the pattern. Refer to the quilt photo for suggestions in choosing fabrics.

Also:
- Cut 9: 4 1/4" x 5 3/8" rectangles, assorted beige plaids
- Cut 12: 1 1/4" x 5 3/8" strips, green plaid
- Cut 1: 4 1/4" x 12" strip, green plaid
- Cut 4: 1 1/4" x 4 1/4" strips, green plaid
- Cut 2: 1 1/4" x 12" strips, black print
- Cut 2: 7/8" x 18 1/8" crosswise strips, black stripe
- Cut 2: 7/8" x 15 1/2" crosswise strips, black stripe
- Cut 3: 1 1/4" x 44" crosswise strips, black stripe, for the binding
- Cut 3: 3/4" x 12" bias strips, black stripe, for the stems

DIRECTIONS
- To prepare the stems, press each 3/4" x 12" black stripe bias strip in thirds, wrong side in, as shown. To reduce bulk, trim 1/8" from each long edge.
- Working on one block at a time and referring to the quilt photo, cut the stem(s) from the prepared bias strips to the desired length and arrange the pieces for each appliqué block on a 4 1/4" x 5 3/8" beige plaid rectangle. Keep the designs centered and clear of the seam allowances (except for the end of each stem which runs off the bottom of the block).
- Notice that the stems are appliquéd first in blocks 2, 3, 4, 5, and 6. The leaves are appliquéd first in blocks 1, 7, 8, and 9. Use traditional appliqué for the stems. Fuse the remaining shapes and embroider a blanket stitch around them using 2 strands of black embroidery floss.

ASSEMBLY
- Lay out the blocks in 3 rows of 3 with 1 1/4" x 5 3/8" green plaid strips between them and at each end. Stitch the blocks and strips into rows.
- Stitch a 4 1/4" x 12" green plaid strip between the 1 1/4" x 12" black print strips along their length to form a pieced strip.
- Cut eight 1 1/4" slices from the pieced strip.
- Stitch a 1 1/4" x 4 1/4" green plaid strip between 2 slices, as shown, to form a pieced sashing. Make 4.

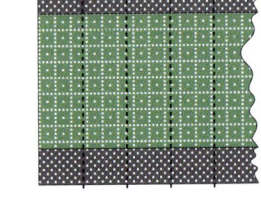

- Lay out the rows with the pieced sashings between them

I used a heart button to indicate my own house in **"Mine Home Is Where Mine Heart Is."** You may want to chose fabrics and threads to produce a folk-art look like I did. The plaids used in this quilt are thicker than the average quilting cotton, giving the houses a rustic look. Use thick thread for the quilting, along with relatively large stitches, to reinforce the effect.

Blanket Stitch

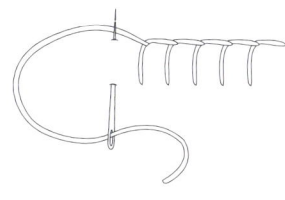

and at the top and bottom. Join the rows and sashings.
• Stitch the 7/8" x 18 1/8" black stripe strips to the sides of the quilt.
• Stitch the 7/8" x 15 1/2" black stripe strips to the top and bottom of the quilt.

For the pieced borders:
Follow the foundation-piecing instructions in the General Directions *to piece the House blocks.*
• Trace the full-size house pattern (page 30) 34 times on the foundation paper, transferring all lines and numbers. Cut each foundation out on the outer lines.

For each House Foundation:
• Piece each block in numerical order using the following fabrics in these positions:
　1 - first print or plaid
　2 - black print
　3, 4 - first print or plaid
　5 - second print or plaid
　6, 7 - light print
• Trim the fabric 1/4" beyond the edges of each foundation.
• Lay out 2 vertical rows of 7 blocks for the side borders.
• Join the blocks in each row and stitch them to the sides of the quilt.
• Lay out 2 horizontal rows of 10 blocks.
• Join the blocks in each row and stitch them to the top and bottom of the quilt.
• Gently remove the paper foundations now.
• Finish the quilt according to the *General Directions*, using the 1 1/4" x 44" black stripe strips for the binding. Embellish the appliqué blocks with the assorted buttons tied on with brown embroidery floss. Refer to the pattern pieces for button placement. Attach the heart button to one of the houses in the same manner.
　　　　　　　　　　　　(The patterns are on pages 29 and 30.)

My Dutch Neighborhood

Mijn Hollands Buurtje

Gather your favorite plaids for a trip around the block!

MATERIALS

- Assorted light print scraps
- Assorted blue print scraps
- Assorted red print scraps for the roofs
- Light plaid at least 8 1/2" square
- 1/8 yard blue and red plaid
- 17" square of backing fabric
- 17" square of thin batting
- Black embroidery floss
- Fusible web

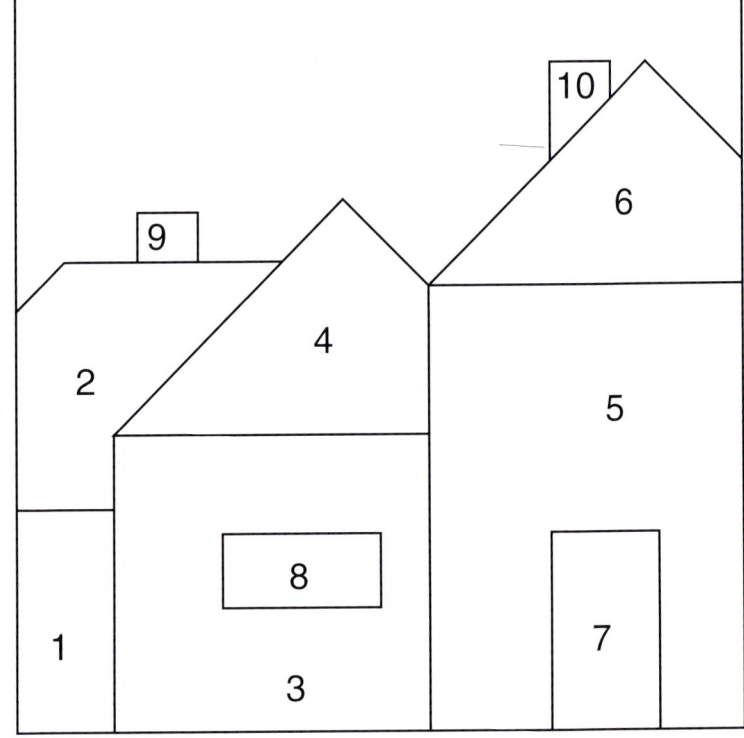

QUILT SIZE: 14 1/2" square
HOUSE BLOCK SIZE: 3 7/8" square
STAR BLOCK SIZE: 2" square

CUTTING

Pattern pieces (here and on page 30) for fusible appliqué are full size and do not need a turn-under allowance. Trace each pattern on the paper side of the fusible web. Rough cut around the traced shapes. Following the manufacturer's directions, fuse the shapes to the wrong side of appropriate fabric scraps. Cut the pieces out on the lines. All other dimensions include a 1/4" seam allowance.

For each of 24 Star blocks:
Group the pieces for each Star block as you cut them.
- Cut 4: 1" squares, light print
- Cut 4: 1" x 1 1/2" rectangles, same light print
- Cut 1: 1 1/2" square, blue print
- Cut 8: 1" squares, same blue print

Also:
- Cut 4: 4 3/8" squares, light plaid, for block backgrounds
- Cut 69: 1 1/4" squares, assorted blue prints
- Cut 2: 1 1/4" x 44" strips, blue and red plaid, for the binding

DIRECTIONS

- Using a light box or a brightly lit window, center and lightly trace the full-size appliqué designs on the right side of the 4 3/8" light plaid squares.
- Following the manufacturer's directions, fuse the fabric pieces for the houses, roofs, doors, and windows onto the 4 3/8" light plaid squares, using the traced pattern as a guide.
- Embroider a blanket stitch around each piece using 2 strands of black floss.
- Stitching with a scant 1/4" seam allowance, join five 1 1/4" assorted blue print squares to make a short sashing row. Press the seam allowances in one direction then measure the row. It should measure 4 3/8". Adjust the seam allowances, if necessary, to make the row that length. Make 6.
- In the same manner, join thirteen 1 1/4" assorted blue print squares to make a long sashing row. Press the seam allowances and measure the row. It should measure 10 1/2". Adjust the seam allowances, if necessary. Make 3.
- Lay out 2 house blocks and 3 short sashing rows, as shown. Join the blocks and sashing rows to make a vertical house row. Make 2.
- Stitch a long sashing row between the house rows. Then stitch one on each side.

For each Star block:
- Draw a diagonal line from corner

It's easier than you think to stitch this charming mini. Fusible appliqué makes it a snap. Use a variety of plaids, checks, stripes, and small prints in your own charming "neighborhood."

Stephen J. Appel Photography

Blanket Stitch

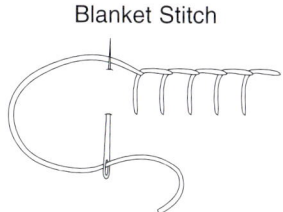

to corner on the wrong side of each 1" blue print square.
• Place a blue print square on one end of a 1" x 1 1/2" light print rectangle, right sides together. Stitch on the drawn line, as shown.

• Press the square toward the corner, aligning the edges. Trim the seam allowance to 1/8". Make 4.
• Lay a 1" blue print square on the opposite end of the light print rectangle and stitch on the drawn line.

• Press and trim, as before, to complete a Star Point unit. Make 4.
• Lay out a 1 1/2" blue print square, 4 Star Point units, and four 1" light print squares, as shown.

• Stitch the units into horizontal rows and join the rows to complete a Star block. Make 24.
• Lay out 5 Star blocks and join them to form a short border. Make 2.

• Lay out 7 Star blocks and join them to form a long border. Make 2.
• Stitch the short borders to the top and bottom of the quilt.
• Stitch the long borders to the sides of the quilt.
• Finish the quilt according to the *General Directions*, using the 1 1/4" x 44" blue and red plaid strips for the binding.

(The patterns are continued on page 30.)

7

Indian Wedding Ring

Make a favorite traditional design with a distinct look.

MATERIALS
- 1/2 yard light print
- 3/4 yard gray plaid
- Fat quarter (18" x 22") peach plaid
- 16" square of backing fabric
- 16" square of thin batting
- Paper for the foundations

QUILT SIZE: 13 3/4" square

CUTTING
Patterns for foundation piecing are full size and do not include a seam allowance. Fabric for foundation piecing will be cut as you stitch the blocks. Each piece must be at least 1/2" larger on all sides than the section it will cover. Refer to the General Directions, *as needed. Patterns for traditional piecing are full-size and include a 1/4" seam allowance.*
- Cut 3: 1 1/4" x 22" bias strips, gray plaid, for the binding
- Cut 24: A, peach plaid
- Cut 9: B, peach plaid

DIRECTIONS
Follow the foundation-piecing instructions in the General Directions *to piece the arcs. Trim the seam allowances to 1/8" after pressing.*
- Trace each full-size arc foundation 24 times on the foundation paper, transferring all lines and numbers. Cut each foundation out on the outer lines.
- Piece each foundation in numerical order using the following fabrics in these positions:

For each Arc 1:
   1 - gray plaid
   2 - light print
   3 - gray plaid
   4 - light print
   5 through 11 - Continue in the established pattern to complete Arc 1. Make 24.

For each Arc 2:
   1 - light print
   2 - gray plaid
   3 - light print
   4 - gray plaid
   5 through 13 - Continue in the established pattern to complete Arc 2. Make 24.

- Trim the fabric 1/4" beyond the edges of each foundation.
- Stitch a peach plaid A to an Arc 1 to make a pieced unit, as shown. Make 24.
- Stitch an Arc 2 to a pieced unit to make a melon, as shown. Make 24.

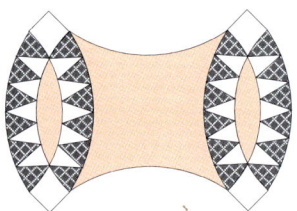

- Stitch melons to opposite sides of a B to make a pieced unit. Make 4.

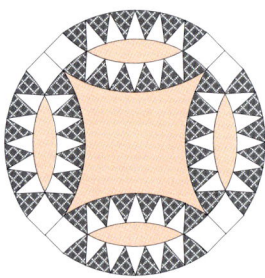

- Stitch melons to the remaining sides of a pieced unit to make a pieced circle. Make 4. Set them aside.

- Stitch melons to 2 adjacent sides of a B to make a corner unit, as shown. Make 4.

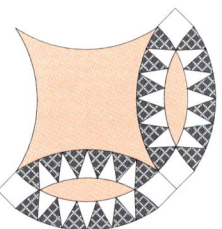

- Lay out the pieced circles, corner units, and remaining B, as shown in the Assembly Diagram on page 9.
- Stitch the units into rows and join the rows.
- Gently remove the paper foundations now.
- Finish the quilt according to the *General Directions*, using the 1 1/4" x 22" gray plaid bias strips for the binding.

This impressive traditional quilt was a winner in the Miniatures from the Heart Contest sponsored annually by *Miniature Quilts* magazine. Whether you make your version to enter in a contest or simply for personal enjoyment, you're certain to be pleased with your **"Indian Wedding Ring."**

Full-Size Patterns and Foundations for Indian Wedding Ring

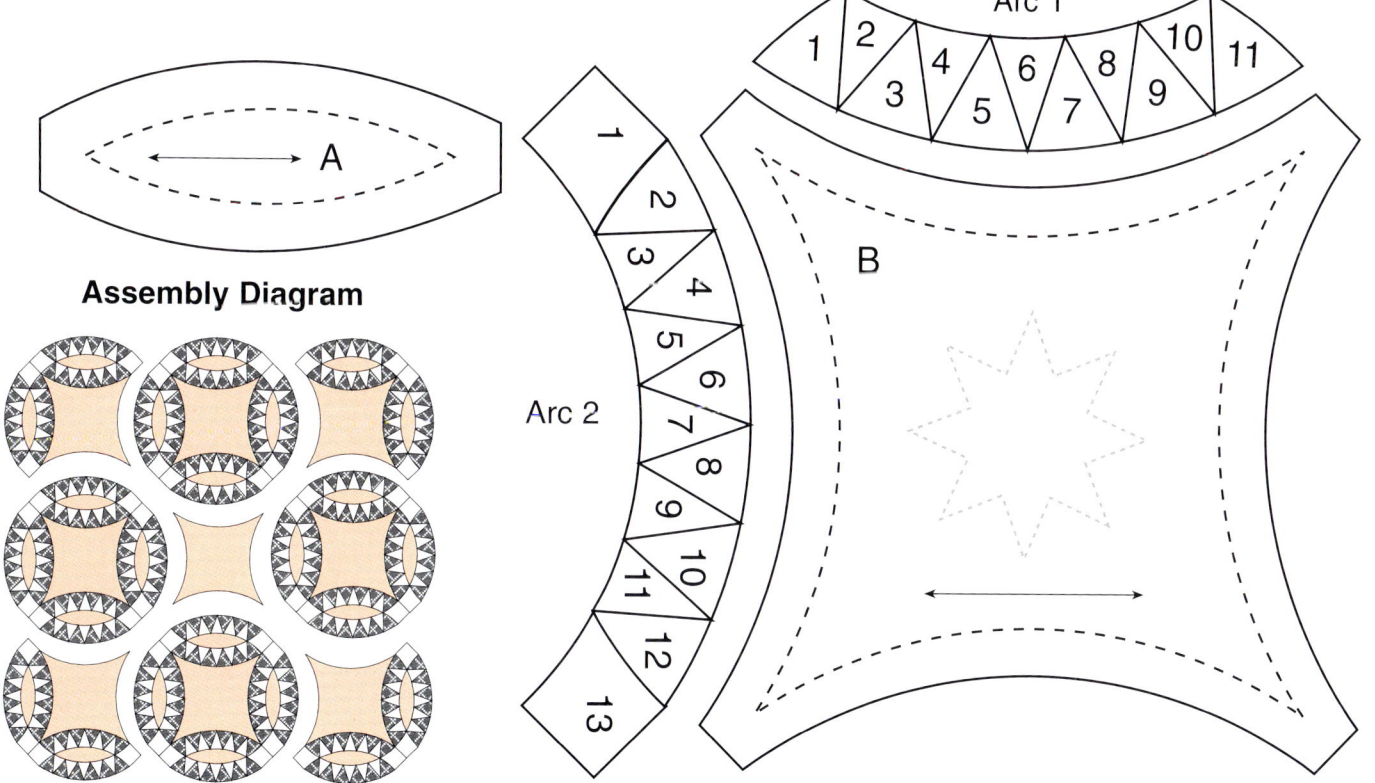

Assembly Diagram

Pots and Plants

Potten en Planten

Create your own potted-garden quilt.

MATERIALS

- Assorted tan and brown prints, each at least 1 1/4" x 13" and totaling 3/8 yard, for the block backgrounds
- 9 assorted clay-colored prints, each at least 2 1/2" square, for the pots
- Assorted prints for flowers and leaves
- Assorted brown plaids, totaling 3/8 yard, for the outer borders
- 1/2 yard green print
- 1/4 yard brown plaid for the binding
- 21" square of backing fabric
- 21" square of thin batting
- Assorted buttons (optional)
- Freezer paper

QUILT SIZE: 18 3/4" square
BLOCK SIZE: 3 3/4" square

CUTTING

Appliqué pattern pieces (page 27) are full size and do not include a turn-under allowance. Trace the pattern pieces on the dull side of the freezer paper. Cut them out on the drawn lines. Iron the freezer paper templates, shiny side down, to the right side of selected fabrics. Use a pencil to lightly trace along the edge of the templates. This is your stitching line. Remove the freezer paper and cut out the fabric shapes adding a 1/8" to 3/16" turn-under allowance. All other dimensions include a 1/4" seam allowance. NOTE: The blocks are numbered 1 through 9, starting in the top left corner and working left to right in each row.

Cut the following for Block 1 and again for Block 8:
- Cut 1: C, first print
- Cut 1: D, second print; or use a button
- Cut 2: E, third print

Cut the following for Block 2 and again for Block 9:
- Cut 1: H, first print
- Cut 1: H, second print
- Cut 1: HR, second print
- Cut 2: I, third print

Cut the following for Block 3 and again for Block 4:
- Cut 5: F, first print
- Cut 2: G, second print

Cut the following for Block 5 and again for Block 7:
- Cut 3: J, first print
- Cut 2: K, second print

Cut the following for Block 6:
- Cut 1: L, first print
- Cut 2: M, second print

Also:
- Cut 9: A, assorted clay prints
- Cut 9: B, matching clay prints
- Cut 25: 1 1/4" x 13" strips, assorted tan and brown prints
- Cut 1: 18" square, green print, then cut five 3/4"-wide bias strips from it, and join them to make a pieced bias strip at least 90" long
- Cut 4: 1 1/4" x 13 1/4" strips, green print
- Cut 6: 1 1/4" x 4 1/4" strips, green print
- Cut 2: 1 1/4" x 16" strips, green print
- Cut 2 1/2"-wide strips, assorted brown plaids of various lengths from 1 3/4" to 3" to total at least 70" in length when joined, for the outer border
- Cut 2: 1 1/4" x 44" strips, brown plaid, for the binding

PREPARATION

- Stitch five 1 1/4" x 13" assorted tan and brown strips, right sides together along their length. Press the seam allowances in one direction. Make 5, changing the placement of the prints in each panel.
- Cut nine 1 1/4" slices from each panel.

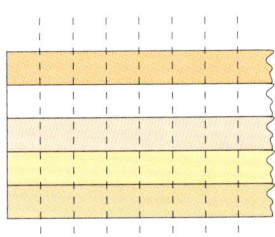

- Stitch 5 slices cut from different panels together to make a background square. Make 9.

DIRECTIONS

Working in alphabetical order and referring to the quilt photo

A fun quilt to make, **"Pots and Plants"** combines plaids, prints, and appliqué to bring a touch of the garden inside. I like to work with plaids, and they certainly add to the warm feel of this country-style quilt.

for placement, needleturn appliqué the flower pieces on the background blocks. It is not necessary to turn edges under or to stitch where pieces will be overlapped by other appliqué pieces.
For each appliqué block:
- Center an A so that the bottom of the flower pot will be about 1/2" from the bottom edge of a background square after it is appliquéd. Pin it in place. Needleturn appliqué the A in place.
- Center and appliqué a B piece to the top of and overlapping the A piece. Make 9.
- Referring to the photo, appliqué the remaining pieces for the blocks.

ASSEMBLY
- Lay out the blocks in 3 horizontal rows of 3 with the 1 1/4" x 4 1/4" green print strips between the blocks in each row.
- Stitch the blocks and strips into rows.
- Lay out the rows with the 1 1/4" x 13 1/4" green print strips between them and at the top and bottom. Join the rows and strips.
- Measure the length of the quilt. Trim the 1 1/4" x 16" green print strips to that measurement. Stitch them to the sides of the quilt.
- Stitch the 2 1/2"-wide assorted brown plaid strips together, end to end, to make a pieced strip at least 70" in length.
- Measure the width of the quilt. Trim 2 lengths from the pieced strip, each equal to that measurement. Be sure there are no seams within 1" of the ends of the strips. Stitch them to the top and bottom of the quilt.
- Measure the length of the quilt, including the borders. Trim 2 lengths from the pieced strip, each equal to that measurement. Stitch them to the sides of the quilt.
- Referring to the photo, lightly mark the placement of the vine on the border.
- Press under a 1/4" seam allowance on both long edges of the 3/4"-wide green print bias strip. Trim 1/8" from each edge to reduce bulk. Appliqué it in place along the vine markings.
- Finish the quilt according to the *General Directions*, using the 1 1/4" x 44" brown plaid strips for the binding.

(The patterns are on page 27.)

Plaids Ruitjes

Piecing these tiny Flying Geese blocks is easy with foundations.

MATERIALS

- Assorted dark plaids, each at least 5 1/4" square
- Assorted light plaids, each at least 4 1/2" square
- 1/8 yard red plaid for the binding
- 12" x 14" piece of backing fabric
- 12" x 14" piece of thin batting
- Paper for the foundations

QUILT SIZE: 9 1/2" x 11 3/4"
BLOCK SIZE: 2 1/4" square

CUTTING

Patterns for foundation piecing are full size and do not include a seam allowance. Fabric for foundation piecing will be cut as you stitch the blocks. Each piece should be at least 1/2" larger on all sides than the section it will cover. Refer to the General Directions, *as needed. All other dimensions include a 1/4" seam allowance.*

- Cut 2: 1 1/4" x 25" strips, red plaid, for the binding

DIRECTIONS

Follow the foundation-piecing instructions in the General Directions *to piece the blocks.*

- Trace the full-size pattern (shown below) 20 times on the foundation paper, transferring all lines and numbers. Cut each foundation out on the outer lines.

For each block:
NOTE: *Choose one dark plaid and 2 light plaids for each block.*

- Piece each foundation in numerical order using the following fabrics in these positions:
    1 - dark plaid
    2, 3 - first light plaid
    4 - dark plaid
    5, 6 - first light plaid
    7 - dark plaid
    8, 9 - first light plaid
    10 - dark plaid
    11, 12 - first light plaid
    13, 14 - dark plaid
    15, 16 - second light plaid
- Trim the fabric 1/4" beyond the edges of each foundation.
- Referring to the photo, lay out the blocks in 5 rows of 4.
- Stitch the blocks into rows and join the rows.
- Gently remove the paper foundations now.
- Finish the quilt according to the *General Directions*, using the 1 1/4" x 25" red plaid strips for the binding.

Full-Size Foundation Pattern for Bigger Plaids

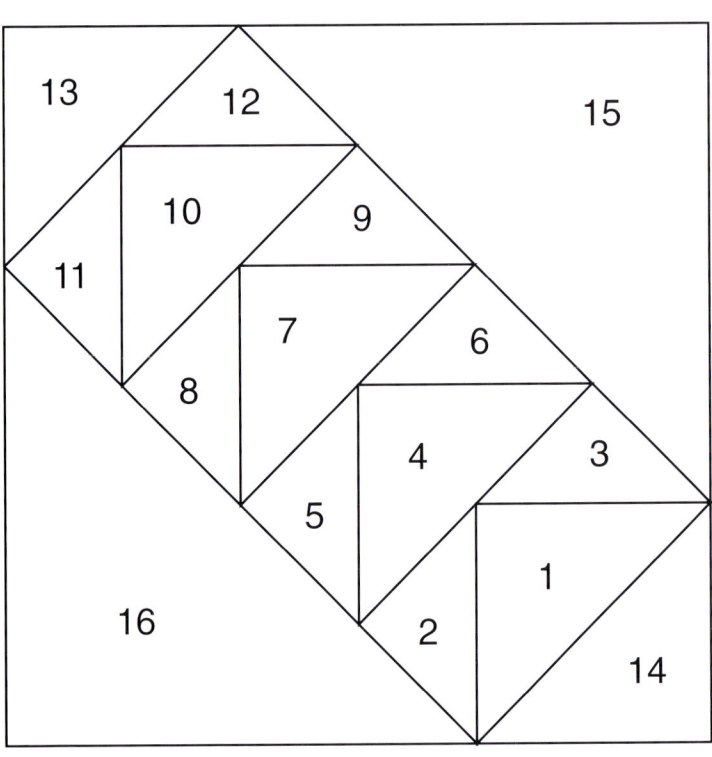

Full-Size Foundation Pattern for Plaids

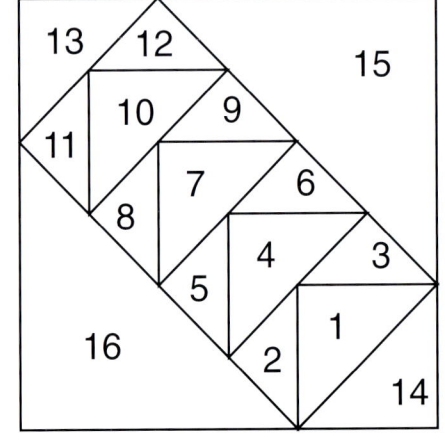

I designed **"Plaids"** for a "Mini of the month" club project. Each month I teach students how to make a miniature quilt using a different technique. This foundation-pieced example is made entirely of plaids for a scrappy country look.

Bigger Plaids

For a larger version of "Plaids," use the following Materials and Cutting lists:

QUILT SIZE: 16 1/2" x 20 1/2"
BLOCK SIZE: 4" square

MATERIALS
- Assorted dark plaids, each at least 7" square
- Assorted light plaids, each at least 7" square
- 1/8 yard red plaid for the binding
- 19" x 23" piece of backing fabric
- 19" x 23" piece of thin batting
- Paper for the foundations

CUTTING
- Cut 2: 1 1/4" x 44" strips, red plaid, for the binding

Follow the **DIRECTIONS** on page 12 to stitch the quilt.

Lily
Lelie

Look at what you can do with just three fabrics!

MATERIALS
- 1/4 yard gold print
- 1/2 yard muslin print
- 1/4 yard brown print
- 16" x 20" piece of backing fabric
- 16" x 20" piece of thin batting

QUILT SIZE: 13 1/2" x 17 1/2"
BLOCK SIZE: 2 7/8" square

CUTTING
Dimensions include a 1/4" seam allowance.
- Cut 12: 2 1/8" squares, gold print, then cut them in half diagonally to yield 24 triangles
- Cut 1: 7/8" x 7" strip, gold print
- Cut 2: 2 1/4" x 19" strips, gold print
- Cut 2: 2 1/4" x 15" strips, gold print
- Cut 2: 3/4" x 19" strips, muslin print
- Cut 2: 3/4" x 15" strips, muslin print
- Cut 2: 1 3/4" x 7" strips, muslin print
- Cut 2: 5 3/8" squares, muslin print, then cut them in quarters diagonally to yield 8 setting triangles. You will use 6.
- Cut 2: 3" squares, muslin print, then cut them in quarters diagonally to yield 4 corner triangles
- Cut 2: 3 3/8" squares, muslin print
- Cut 3: 3" squares, muslin print
- Cut 12: 7/8" x 1 3/4" strips, muslin print
- Cut 24: 1 1/8" squares, muslin print
- Cut 3: 3" squares, brown print
- Cut 2: 7/8" x 19" strips, brown print
- Cut 2: 7/8" x 15" strips, brown print
- Cut 4: 1 1/4" x 44" strips, brown print, for the binding

DIRECTIONS
Trim the seam allowances to 1/8" after pressing.
- Draw diagonal lines, from corner to corner, on the wrong side of each 3" muslin print square. Draw horizontal and vertical lines through the centers.
- Lay a marked muslin square on a 3" brown print square, right sides together. Stitch 1/4" away from the diagonal lines on both sides, as shown. Make 3.

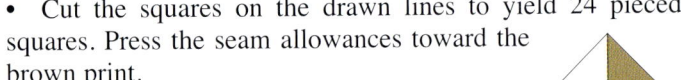

- Cut the squares on the drawn lines to yield 24 pieced squares. Press the seam allowances toward the brown print.
- Cut the pieced squares in half, as shown, to yield 48 pieced triangles.
- Stitch a 1 1/8" muslin print square between 2 pieced triangles, as shown, with the brown print triangles against the muslin square.

- Stitch the unit to a gold print triangle to complete a pieced square. Make 24.

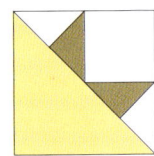

- Stitch a 7/8" x 1 3/4" muslin print strip between 2 pieced squares to make a half-block, as shown. Make 12. Set them aside.

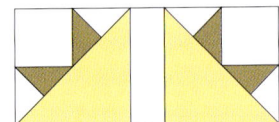

- Stitch a 7/8" x 7" gold print strip between two 1 3/4" x 7" muslin print strips, along their length.
- Cut six 7/8" slices from the pieced strip.

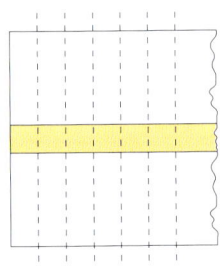

- Stitch a slice between 2 half-blocks, as shown, to complete a block. Make 6.

The light-colored, narrow middle border of "**Lily**" gives this quilt an airy feeling, offsetting the darker borders and binding.

ASSEMBLY

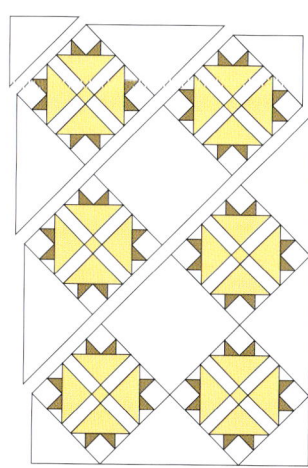

- Referring to the Assembly Diagram, lay out the blocks on point in 3 rows of 2, with the 3 3/8" muslin print squares in the center, muslin print corner triangles in the corners, and muslin print setting triangles along the edges.
- Stitch the blocks, squares, and triangles into diagonal rows and join the rows.
- Stitch a 3/4" x 15" muslin print strip between a 7/8" x 15" brown print strip and a 2 1/4" x 15" gold print strip to make a short pieced border. Make 2.
- In the same manner, make 2 long pieced borders using the 19"-long muslin print, brown print, and gold print strips.
- Center and stitch the long pieced borders to the long sides of the quilt, placing the brown print strips against the quilt. Start, stop, and backstitch 1/4" from the edges of the quilt.
- Stitch the short pieced borders to the short sides of the quilt in the same manner.
- Miter each corner referring to the *General Directions*.
- Finish the quilt according to the *General Directions*, using the 1 1/4" x 44" brown print strips for the binding.

(The full-size Quilting Design is on page 25.)

15

Black Spider — Zwarte Spin

Piece this mini using the classic Anvil block.

MATERIALS
- 1/2 yard red print
- 1/3 yard black print
- 16" x 19" piece of backing fabric
- 16" x 19" piece of thin batting

QUILT SIZE: 13 1/2" x 16 1/2"
BLOCK SIZE: 2 1/2" square

CUTTING
Patterns (page 19) for foundation piecing are full size and do not include a seam allowance. Fabric for foundation piecing will be cut as you stitch the border. Each piece should be at least 1/2" larger on all sides than the section it will cover. Refer to the General Directions, *as needed. All other dimensions include a 1/4" seam allowance.*
- Cut 2: 1 1/4" x 44" strips, black print, for the binding
- Cut 15: 3" squares, black print
- Cut 12: 1 3/4" squares, black print
- Cut 6: 1 1/8" squares, black print
- Cut 15: 3" squares, red print
- Cut 24: 1 1/8" squares, red print
- Cut 17: 1 1/8" x 3" strips, red print
- Cut 2: 1 7/8" squares, red print, then cut them in half diagonally to yield 4 triangles
- Cut 2: 1 1/8" x 9 1/4" strips, red print, for the inner border
- Cut 2: 1 1/8" x 13 5/8" strips, red print, for the inner border
- Cut 2: 1 3/4" x 12" strips, red print, for the outer border
- Cut 2: 1 3/4" x 18" strips, red print, for the outer border

DIRECTIONS
Trim the seam allowances to 1/8" after pressing.
- Draw diagonal lines from corner to corner on the wrong side of each 3" red print square. Draw horizontal and vertical lines through the centers.
- Place a marked red print square on a 3" black print square, right sides together. Sew 1/4" away from the diagonal lines on both sides, as shown. Make 15.

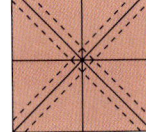

- Cut the squares on the drawn lines to yield 120 pieced squares. Press the seam allowances toward the black print.
- Lay out a 1 1/8" red print square and 3 pieced squares, as shown. Stitch them together to form a pieced row. Make 24.

- Stitch 2 pieced squares together to form a pieced rectangle, as shown. Make 24.
- Stitch pieced rectangles to opposite sides of a 1 3/4" black print square to make a center unit, as shown. Make 12.

- Stitch 2 pieced rows to a center unit to complete a Black Spider block, as shown. Make 12.

- Stitch three 1 1/8" x 3" red print strips and two 1 1/8" black print squares together to form a pieced sashing strip. Make 3.

ASSEMBLY
- Lay out the blocks, remaining 1 1/8" x 3" red print strips, and pieced sashing strips, as shown.

- Stitch the blocks and 1 1/8" x 3" red print strips into rows.
- Join the rows and pieced sashing strips.
- Stitch the 1 1/8" x 9 1/4" red print strips to the short sides of the quilt.
- Stitch the 1 1/8" x 13 5/8" red print strips to the long sides of the quilt.

You can stitch a precision-pieced little quilt like **"Black Spider."** Even though it contains only two colors, this quilt is sure to make a bold statement in your home.

For the borders:

Follow the foundation-piecing instructions in the General Directions *to piece the borders.*

- Trace the Short Border pattern (page 19) twice on the foundation paper, transferring all lines. Make a long Border Foundation by tracing the partial pattern and extending it to include 14 dark triangles and 13 light ones. Make 2. Cut each foundation out on the outer lines.
- Piece each foundation using black print in the shaded sections and red print in the unshaded sections.
- Trim the fabric 1/4" beyond the edges of each foundation.
- Stitch the short foundation-pieced borders to the short sides of the quilt, placing the black print triangles against the quilt.
- Stitch the long foundation-pieced borders to the long sides of the quilt in the same manner.
- Stitch a red print triangle to each corner, as shown.
- Measure the width of the quilt. Trim the 1 3/4" x 12" red print strips to that measurement. Stitch them to the short sides of the quilt.
- Measure the length of the quilt, including the borders. Trim the 1 3/4" x 18" red print strips to that measurement. Stitch them to the remaining sides of the quilt.
- Gently remove the paper foundations now.
- Finish the quilt according to the *General Directions*, using the 1 1/4" x 44" black print strips for the binding.

(The patterns are on page 19.)

Happy Spools

Vrolijke Klossen

Waste not, want not—make clever use of every inch of your fabric!

MATERIALS

- Assorted print scraps, each at least 1 1/2" square, for the spool centers
- Assorted selvage strips which display company names
- Assorted print strips in various widths from 3/4" to 1 1/2" and at least 1 3/4" in length, for the pieced sashings and borders
- Assorted 1 1/4"-wide print strips in various lengths for the binding
- 1/4 yard tan check
- 1/8 yard brown print
- 15" x 18" piece of backing fabric
- 15" x 18" piece of thin batting
- Needle and thread for embellishment

QUILT SIZE: 13" x 16"

CUTTING

Appliqué pattern pieces are full size and do not include a turn-under allowance. Make templates for each of the pieces. Trace around the templates on the right side of the fabric and add a 1/8" turn-under allowance when cutting the pieces out. **NOTE:** *The seam allowance for piecing the spools is also 1/8". The selvage strips that contain a company name may need to be stitched with a 1/8" seam allowance so that the writing will remain visible on the quilt top. All other dimensions include a 1/4" seam allowance.*

- Cut 15: A, assorted prints
- Cut 34: C, assorted prints
- Cut 30: B, brown print
- Cut 68: D, brown print
- Cut 3: 2 1/2" x 11 1/2" strips, tan check, for the center strips
- Cut 2: 2 1/8" x 10 1/4" strips, tan check, for the top and bottom borders
- Cut 2: 1 7/8" x 16" strips, tan check, for the side borders
- Cut 1 1/4"-wide print strips equivalent to 70" in length when joined end to end, for the binding

DIRECTIONS

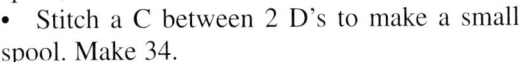

- Stitch an A between 2 B's to make a large spool, as shown. Make 15.
- Stitch a C between 2 D's to make a small spool. Make 34.
- Referring to the photo, appliqué 5 large spools to a 2 1/2" x 11 1/2" tan check strip keeping the spools at least 1/4" away from the edges of the strip. Make 3. Set them aside.
- Stitch enough selvage strips and print strips together to make a pieced sashing strip that measures 1 3/4" x 11 1/2". Make 2.

NOTE: *The writing on selvage strips makes them directional, so place them in one direction as you stitch the quilt.*

- Lay out the appliquéd strips and the pieced sashing strips, as shown. Join the strips.

- Stitch selvage strips and print strips together to make 2 pieced border strips that measure 1 1/8" x 11 1/2".
- Stitch them to the sides of the quilt.
- Stitch selvage strips and print strips together to make 2 pieced border strips that measure 1 1/8" x 10 1/4".
- Stitch them to the top and bottom of the quilt.
- Appliqué 7 small spools to a 2 1/8" x 10 1/4" tan check strip, as shown, leaving a 1/4" seam allowance around the edges, as before. Make 2 of these horizontal borders.

"**Happy Spools**" provides a perfect way to use those selvage edges that cling to the fabric scraps you just can't toss away. This adorable quilt would make a colorful gift for a special quilting friend or a lively accent for your sewing room.

Full-Size Appliqué Patterns for Happy Spools

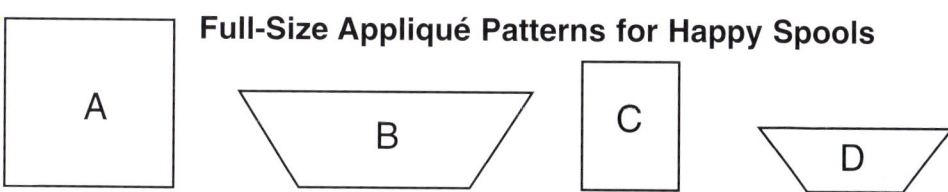

- Stitch them to the top and bottom of the quilt.
- Appliqué 10 small spools to a 1 7/8" x 16" tan check strip to make a vertical border. Make 2.
- Stitch them to the sides of the quilt.
- Stitch the 1 1/4"-wide binding strips together to make a pieced strip.
- Finish the quilt according to the *General Directions*, using the 1 1/4"-wide pieced strip for the binding.
- Insert a threaded needle into the quilt for a finishing touch!

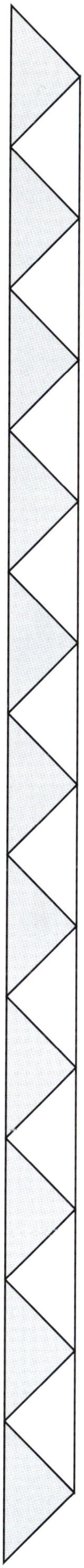

Short Border Foundation

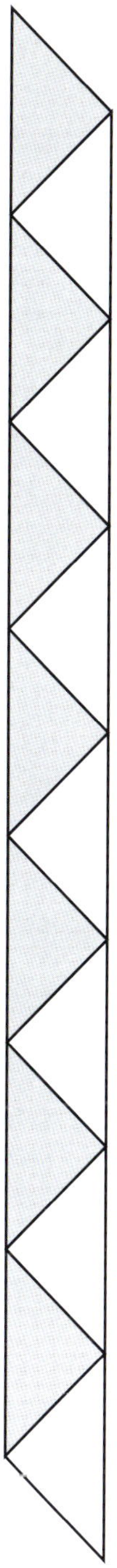

Partial Long Border Foundation

Foundation Patterns for Black Spider
(The pattern begins on page 16.)

Baskets
Mandjes

Use a red check fabric to simulate woven splints in these cute baskets.

MATERIALS

- Fat eighth (11" x 18") light tan print
- Fat eighth medium tan print
- Fat eighth red print
- Fat eighth red check
- 9" x 11" piece of backing fabric
- 9" x 11" piece of thin batting
- Paper for the border foundations (optional)

QUILT SIZE: 6 1/4" x 9"
BLOCK SIZE: 1 1/2" square

CUTTING
Dimensions include a 1/4" seam allowance.
- Cut 24: 7/8" squares, red print
- Cut 24: 1 3/4" squares, red print, then cut them in quarters diagonally to yield 96 triangles for the pieced borders NOTE: *Do not cut these if you choose to foundation piece the borders.*
- Cut 12: 7/8" x 1 1/4" rectangles, light tan print
- Cut 1: 1 1/4" x 12" strip, light tan print
- Cut 6: 7/8" squares, light tan print
- Cut 3: 1 5/8" squares, light tan print, then cut them in half diagonally to yield 6 triangles
- Cut 3: 1 5/8" squares, light tan print
- Cut 2: 2" squares, medium tan print
- Cut 24: 1 3/4" squares, medium tan print, then cut them in quarters diagonally to yield 96 triangles for the pieced borders NOTE: *Do not cut these if you choose to foundation piece the borders. Directions for foundation-pieced borders are on page 23.*
- Cut 2: 2" squares, medium tan print, then cut them in half diagonally to yield 4 corner triangles
- Cut 2: 3 3/8" squares, medium tan print, then cut them in quarters diagonally to yield 8 setting triangles. You will use 6.
- Cut 2: 1" x 9" strips, medium tan print
- Cut 2: 1" x 7" strips, medium tan print
- Cut 3: 1 5/8" squares, red check
- Cut 1: 7/8" x 12" strip, red check
- Cut 2: 1 1/4" x 18" strips, red check, for the binding

DIRECTIONS
Trim the seam allowances to 1/8" after pressing.
- Draw a diagonal line, from corner to corner, on the wrong side of each 1 5/8" light tan print square.
- Lay a marked square on a 1 5/8" red check square, right sides together. Stitch 1/4" away from the diagonal line on both sides. Make 3.

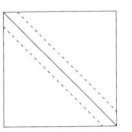

- Cut the squares on the marked lines to yield 6 pieced squares. Press the seam allowances toward the red print. Set them aside.
- Draw a diagonal line from corner to corner on the wrong side of each 7/8" red print square.
- Place a marked red print square on one end of a 7/8" x 1 1/4" light tan print rectangle, right sides together. Stitch on the drawn line, as shown.

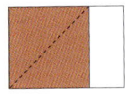

- Press the square toward the corner, aligning the edges. Trim the seam allowance to 1/8".
- Lay a marked red print square on the opposite end of the rectangle and stitch on the drawn line. Press and trim, as before, to complete a Flying Geese unit. Make 12.

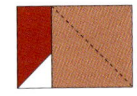

- Lay out 2 Flying Geese units, a pieced square, and a 7/8" light tan print square. Stitch them into sections and join the sections to make a basket unit. Make 6.

- Stitch a 7/8" x 12" red check strip to a 1 1/4" x 12" light tan print strip, along their length.
- Cut twelve 7/8" sections from the pieced strip.

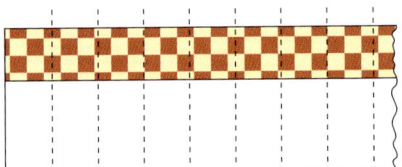

- Stitch sections to a basket unit. Trim the corner of the unit diagonally, as shown, maintaining a 1/4" seam allowance beyond the point of the basket.

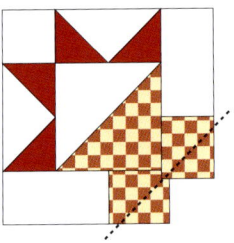

"**Baskets**" illustrates the importance of proportion in designing miniature blocks. Use prints that are small enough not to overwhelm the design, and let the check fabric add detail without additional piecing.

Full-Size Quilting Design for Baskets

- Stitch a light tan print triangle to the trimmed corner to complete a Basket block. Make 6.

ASSEMBLY
- Referring to the photo, lay out the Basket blocks on point in 3 rows of 2. Place 2" medium tan print squares between the blocks, medium tan print corner triangles in the corners, and medium tan print setting triangles along the edges.
- Stitch the blocks, squares, and triangles into diagonal rows and join the rows.
NOTE: *If you prefer to piece the borders on foundations, refer to Foundation-Pieced Borders for Baskets on page 23. For traditional piecing, continue with the directions below.*
- Stitch a red print triangle to a medium tan print triangle to make a border unit. Make 92.
- Lay out 8 border units and a medium tan print triangle. Stitch them together to make a short inner border. Make 2.

- In the same manner, stitch 12 border units and a medium tan print triangle together to make a long inner border. Make 2.
- Stitch 11 border units and a red print triangle together to make a short outer border. Make 2.

- In the same manner, stitch 15 border units and a red print triangle together to make a long outer border. Make 2.
- Center and stitch a short inner border to a 1" x 7" medium tan print trip. Center and stitch a short outer border to the opposite side of the medium tan print strip, as shown. Make 2.

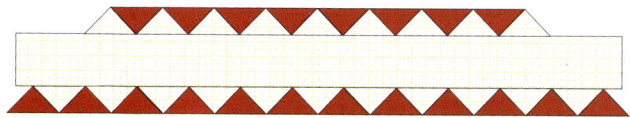

(continued on page 22)

Hearts of Nine
Harten Negen

You can whip up this quilt in a heartbeat.

MATERIALS
- Assorted dark print scraps in red, yellow, blue, and green, each at least 3" square
- Assorted off-white print scraps, each at least 3" square
- Fat eighth (11" x 18") blue print for the border
- Fat eighth red print for the binding
- 18" x 20" piece of backing fabric
- 18" x 20" piece of thin batting
- Fusible web
- Embroidery floss to match or contrast with the appliqué fabrics

Full-Size Appliqué Pattern for Hearts of Nine

QUILT SIZE: 15 3/4" x 18"
BLOCK SIZE: 2 1/4" square

CUTTING
Pattern pieces for fusible appliqué are full size and do not need a turn-under allowance. Trace the pattern on the paper side of the fusible web. Rough cut around the shapes. Following the manufacturer's directions, fuse the shapes to the wrong side of the selected fabrics. Cut them out on the drawn lines. All other dimensions include a 1/4" seam allowance.
- Cut 15: Hearts, assorted red, yellow, blue, and green prints
- Cut 75: 1 1/4" squares, assorted red, yellow, blue, and green prints
- Cut 15: 3" squares, assorted off-white prints
- Cut 60: 1 1/4" squares, assorted off-white prints
- Cut 4: 2 1/2" x 17" strips, blue print
- Cut 5: 1 1/4" x 18" strips, red print, for the binding

DIRECTIONS
- Center a dark print heart in a 3" off-white print square. Following the manufacturer's directions, fuse the heart to the square.
- Embroider a blanket stitch around the heart using 2 strands of matching or contrasting embroidery floss. Make 15.
- Trim the blocks to 2 3/4" square, keeping the heart centered. Set them aside.
- Lay out five 1 1/4" dark print squares alternately with four 1 1/4" off-white print squares in 3 rows of 3, as shown.
- Stitch the squares into rows and join the

Baskets (continued from page 21)

- In the same manner, stitch a long inner border and a long outer border to a 1" x 9" medium tan print strip. Make 2.
- Trim the tan print strips even with the raw edges of the end triangles on each border.

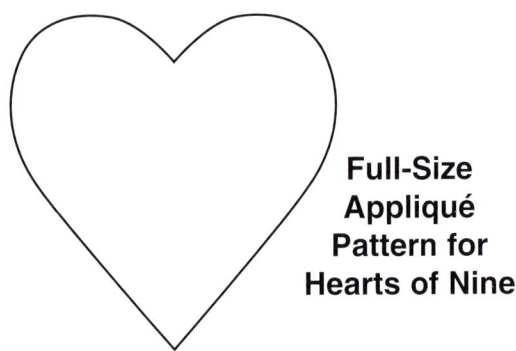

- Center and stitch the short borders to the top and bottom of the quilt. Start, stop, and backstitch 1/4" from the raw edges.
- Center and stitch the long borders to the sides of the quilt in the same manner. Stitch the corner seams to form miters.
- If you used foundations for the borders, gently remove the paper now.
- Finish the quilt according to the *General Directions*, using the 1 1/4" x 18" red check strips for the binding.

Outer Border Foundation

Inner Border Foundation

Border Foundation Patterns for Baskets

I stitched **"Hearts of Nine"** in a scrappy, country mood, accentuated by the blanket stitch used with fusible appliqué. If you prefer, you can needleturn appliqué the hearts for a more traditional look.

Blanket Stitch

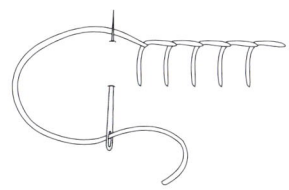

rows to complete a Nine Patch block. Make 15.
- Referring to the photo, lay out the Nine Patch blocks alternately with the Heart blocks in 6 rows of 5.
- Stitch the blocks into rows and join the rows.
- Measure the length of the quilt. Trim 2 of the 2 1/2" x 17" blue print strips to that measurement. Stitch them to the long sides of the quilt.
- Measure the width of the quilt, including the borders. Trim the remaining 2 1/2" x 17" blue print strips to that measurement. Stitch them to the remaining sides of the quilt.
- Finish the quilt according to the *General Directions*, using the 1 1/4" x 18" red print strips for the binding.

 # Foundation-Pieced Borders for Baskets

CUTTING
Patterns for foundation piecing are full size and do not include a seam allowance. Fabric for foundation piecing will be cut as you stitch the borders. Each piece should be at least 1/2" larger on all sides than the section it will cover. Refer to the General Directions *as needed.*

DIRECTIONS
Follow the foundation-piecing instructions in the General Directions *to piece the borders.*
- Trace the Inner Border Foundation twice on the foundation paper, transferring all lines. In addition, make a long Inner Border Foundation by tracing the same pattern and extending it to include 13 light triangles and 12 dark ones. Make 2. Trace the Outer Border Foundation twice. In addition, make a long Outer Border Foundation by tracing the same pattern and extending it to include 16 dark triangles and 15 light ones. Make 2. Cut each foundation out on the outer lines.
- Piece each foundation using red print in the shaded sections and medium tan print in the unshaded sections.
- Trim the fabric 1/4" beyond the edges of each foundation.
- Assemble the quilt as described in the pattern directions.

Sunflowers
Zonnebloemen

These little flowers will make a delightful autumn quilt for your home.

MATERIALS

- Fat eighth (11" x 18") brown print
- Fat eighth yellow print
- Fat eighth green print
- Fat eighth muslin
- Fat eighth dark tan print
- 1/2 yard brown check
- 1/4 yard light tan print
- 15" square of backing fabric
- 15" square of thin batting
- Fusible web
- Yellow, green, and brown embroidery floss

QUILT SIZE: 12 1/2" square
BLOCK SIZE: 3" square

CUTTING

Pattern pieces for fusible appliqué are full size and do not need a turn-under allowance. Trace the patterns on the paper side of the fusible web. Rough cut around the traced shapes. Following the manufacturer's directions, fuse the shapes to the wrong side of the selected fabrics. Cut them out on the drawn lines. All other dimensions include a 1/4" seam allowance. Cut the bias strips from the brown check before cutting the smaller, straight-grain pieces from that fabric.

- Cut 12: A, green print
- Cut 18: D, green print
- Cut 4: B, yellow print
- Cut 12: E, yellow print
- Cut 4: C, brown print
- Cut 12: F, brown print
- Cut 4: 2 1/2" squares, muslin
- Cut 4: 1" x 2 1/2" strips, dark tan print
- Cut 8: 1" x 3" strips, dark tan print
- Cut 4: 1" x 3 1/2" strips, dark tan print
- Cut 4: 2 3/4" x 14" strips, light tan print
- Cut 2: 1" x 3 1/2" strips, brown check
- Cut 3: 1" x 7" strips, brown check
- Cut 2: 1" x 8" strips, brown check
- Cut 4: 1 1/4" x 14" bias strips, brown check, for the binding

DIRECTIONS

- Stitch a 1" x 2 1/2" dark tan print strip to the left side of a 2 1/2" muslin square.
- Stitch a 1" x 3" dark tan print strip to the top of the muslin square, as shown.

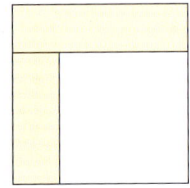

- Stitch a 1" x 3" dark tan print strip to the right side of the muslin square. Stitch a 1" x 3 1/2" dark tan print strip to the bottom to make a pieced block. Make 4.

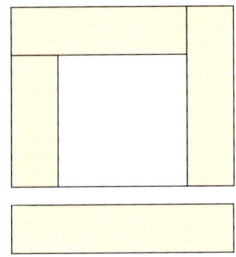

- Referring to the photo for placement, center a large flower (B) in each pieced block. Tuck 3 leaves (A) under each flower. Place a dark brown print C in the center of each large flower.
- Following the manufacturer's directions, fuse the pieces in place.
- Embroider a blanket stitch around each piece using 2 strands of matching embroidery floss.
- Stitch a 1" x 3 1/2" brown check strip between 2 blocks to complete a row. Make 2.
- Lay out the rows with a 1" x 7" brown check strip between them and at the top and bottom. Stitch them together.
- Stitch 1" x 8" brown check strips to the long sides of the quilt.
- Measure the length of the quilt. Trim 2 of the 2 3/4" x 14" light tan print strips to that measurement and stitch them to opposite sides of the quilt.
- Measure the width of the quilt, including the borders. Trim the remaining 2 3/4" x 14" light tan print strips to that measurement and stitch them to the remaining sides of the quilt.
- In the same manner as for the blocks, appliqué 3 small flowers (E, F), with one or 2 leaves (D) each, in the light tan print border along each side of the quilt.
- Finish the quilt according to the *General Directions*, using the 1 1/4" x 14" brown check bias strips for the binding.

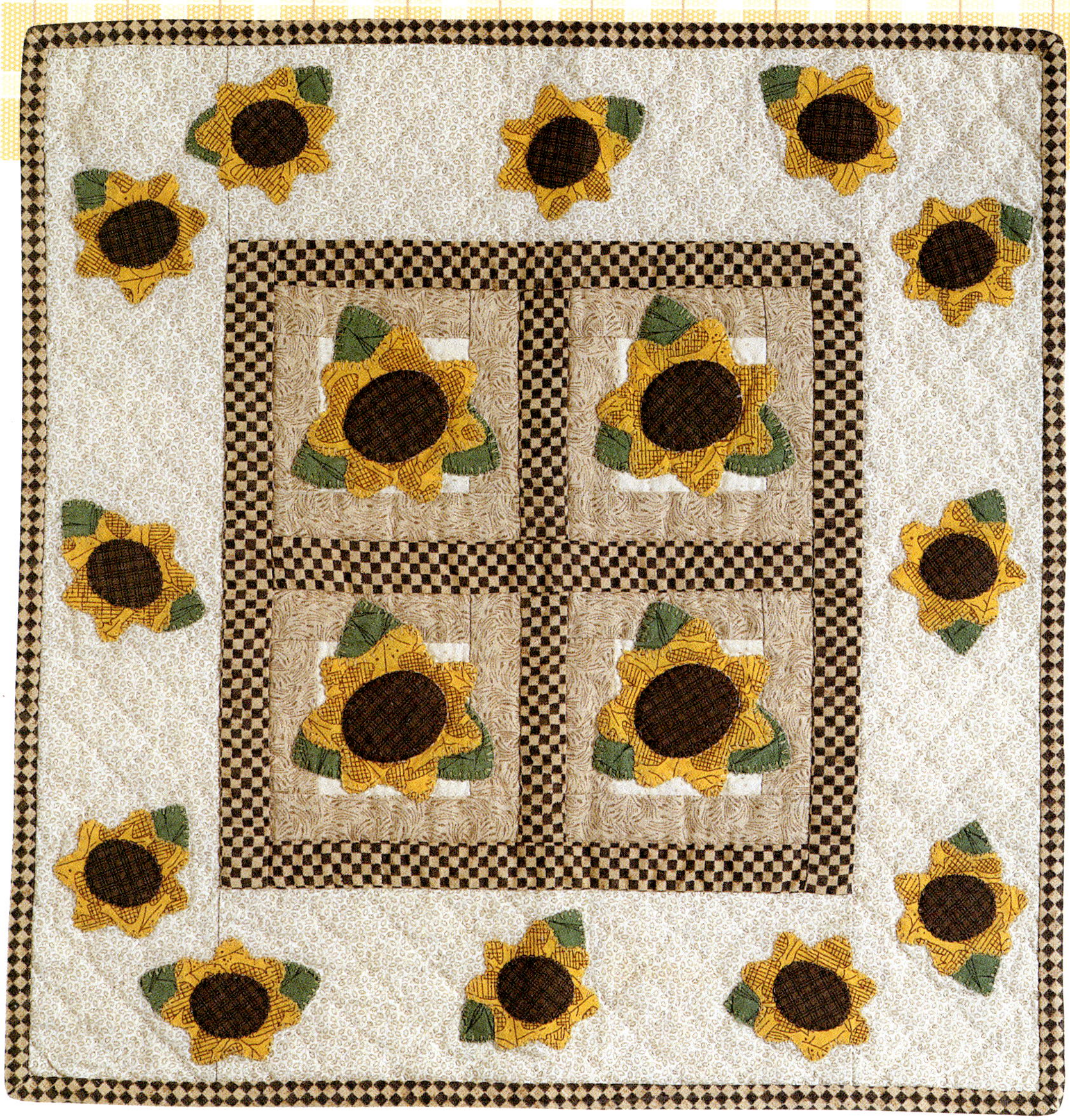

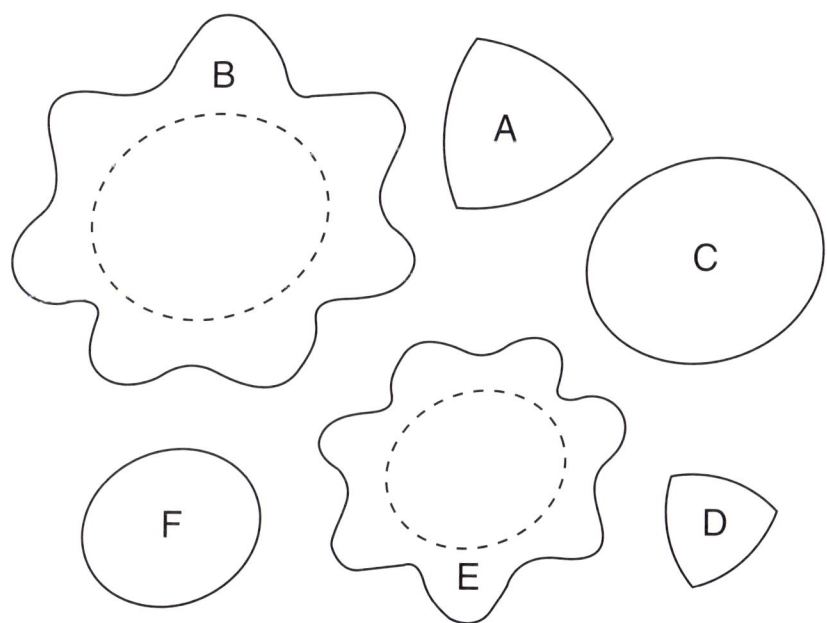

"Sunflowers" begins with traditional log cabin construction but doesn't end there. Appliquéd flowers soften the straight lines of the underlying "architecture."

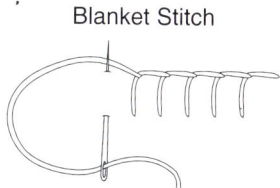

Blanket Stitch

Full-Size Appliqué Patterns for Sunflowers

Full-Size Quilting Design for Lily
(The pattern begins on page 14.)

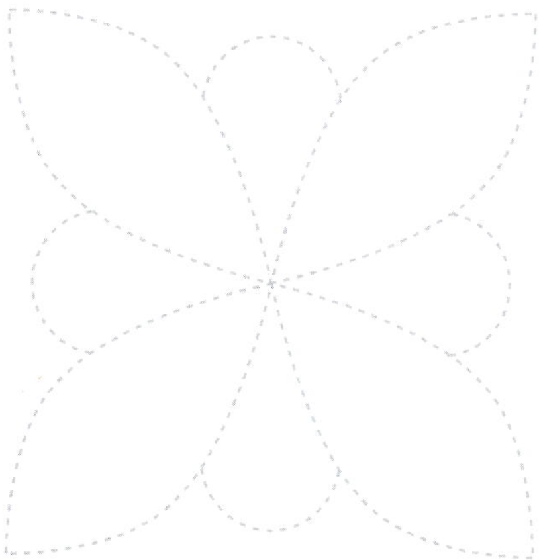

The Wheel of Adventure

Rad van Avontuur

Stage a dramatic presentation with this small quilt.

MATERIALS
- 1/2 yard orange plaid
- Assorted plaid strips ranging in width from 5/8" to 7/8" and totaling 1 1/2 yards, for the blocks
- Assorted 1"-wide plaid strips ranging in length from 4" to 7" and totaling 100", for the middle border
- 2/3 yard black
- 22" square of backing fabric
- 22" square of thin batting
- Paper for the foundations

QUILT SIZE: 20" square
BLOCK SIZE: 3 3/4" square

CUTTING
Patterns for foundation piecing are full size and do not include a seam allowance. Fabric for foundation piecing will be cut as you stitch the blocks. Each piece must be at least 1/4" larger on all sides than the section it will cover. Refer to the General Directions *as needed. All other dimensions include a 1/4" seam allowance.*
- Cut 2: 1 1/4" x 16" strips, black, for the inner border
- Cut 2: 1 1/4" x 18" strips, black, for the inner border
- Cut 2: 1 1/2" x 18 1/2" strips, black, for the outer border
- Cut 2: 1 1/2" x 21" strips, black, for the outer border
- Cut 2: 1 1/4" x 44" strips, black, for the binding

DIRECTIONS
Follow the foundation-piecing instructions in the General Directions *to piece the blocks.*
- Trace the full-size foundation pattern 64 times on the foundation paper, transferring all lines and numbers. Cut each foundation out on the outer lines.

For each foundation:
- Piece each foundation in numerical order using the following fabrics in these positions:
    1 - black
    2, 3 - orange plaid
  Stitch random width plaid strips to the remaining areas of each foundation.

- Trim the fabric 1/4" beyond the edges of each foundation.
- Stitch 4 foundations together, as shown, to complete a block. Make 16.

ASSEMBLY
- Lay out the blocks in 4 rows of 4.
- Stitch the blocks into rows. Join the rows.
- Measure the length of the quilt. Trim the 1 1/4" x 16" black strips to that measurement. Stitch them to opposite sides of the quilt.
- Measure the width of the quilt, including the borders. Trim the 1 1/4" x 18" black strips to the measurement. Stitch them to the remaining sides of the quilt.
- Stitch the assorted 1"-wide plaid strips together, end to end, to make 4 pieced strips, each measuring at least 19" in length.
- Measure the length of the quilt and trim 2 pieced strips to that measurement. Stitch them to opposite sides of the quilt.
- Measure the width of the quilt, including the borders. Trim the remaining pieced strips to that measurement. Stitch them to the remaining sides of the quilt.
- In the same manner, trim the 1 1/2" x 18 1/2" black strips to fit the quilt's length and stitch them to opposite sides of the quilt.
- Trim the 1 1/2" x 21" black strips to fit the quilt's width and stitch them to the remaining sides of the quilt.
- Gently remove the paper foundations now.
- Finish the quilt according to the *General Directions*, using the 1 1/4" x 44" black strips for the binding.

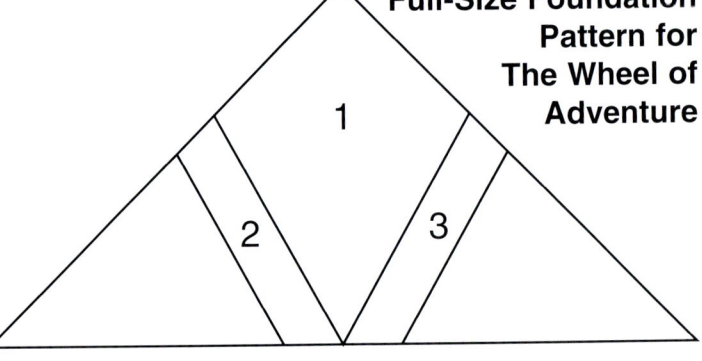

Full-Size Foundation Pattern for The Wheel of Adventure

I originally designed **"The Wheel of Adventure"** for a miniature-of-the-month class that I teach. Now you can make it too! This is a great way to use plaid scraps.

Full-Size Appliqué Patterns for Pots and Plants

(The pattern begins on page 10.)

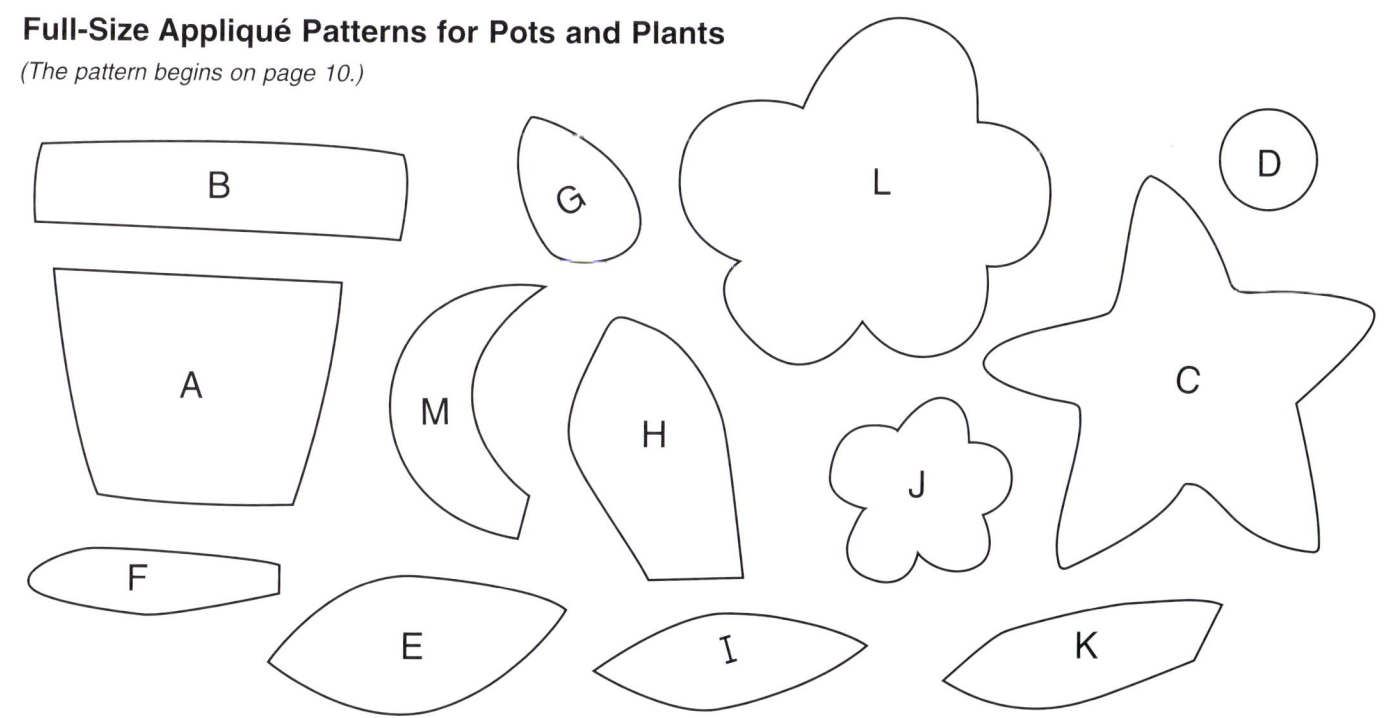

Mystery Stars

Mysterie Sterren

It's really no mystery—these little stars spark up a quilt in a twinkle.

MATERIALS

- Assorted medium and dark prints, each at least 3 1/2" square
- 1/6 yard muslin
- Fat eighth (11" x 18") gold plaid for the inner border
- Fat eighth green plaid for the outer border and binding
- Red print at least 4 1/2" square, for the corner squares
- 15" square of backing fabric
- 15" square of thin batting

QUILT SIZE: 12 1/4" square
BLOCK SIZE: 2 1/2" square

CUTTING

Dimensions include a 1/4" seam allowance.

For each of 9 Star blocks:
- Cut 1: 1 3/4" square, medium or dark print, for the Star center
- Cut 8: 1 1/8" squares, contrasting print, for the Star points

Also:
- Cut 36: 1 1/8" x 1 3/4" rectangles, muslin
- Cut 36: 1 1/8" squares, muslin
- Cut 2: 7/8" x 8 3/4" strips, gold plaid, for the inner border
- Cut 2: 7/8" x 8" strips, gold plaid, for the inner border
- Cut 4: 2 1/4" x 8 3/4" strips, green plaid, for the outer border
- Cut 3: 1 1/4" x 18" strips, green plaid, for the binding
- Cut 4: 2 1/4" squares, red print

DIRECTIONS

For each Star block:
- Draw a diagonal line from corner to corner on the wrong side of each 1 1/8" print square.
- Place a marked square on one end of a 1 1/8" x 1 3/4" muslin rectangle, right sides together. Stitch on the marked line, as shown.
- Press the square toward the corner, aligning the raw edges. Trim the seam allowance 1/8" beyond the stitching.
- Place a matching 1 1/8" square on the opposite end of the rectangle. Stitch, press, and trim, as before, to complete a Star point unit. Make 4.

- Lay out a 1 3/4" print center square, 4 Star point units, and four 1 1/8" muslin squares. Stitch them into rows and join the rows to complete a Star block. Make 9.

ASSEMBLY

- Lay out the blocks in 3 rows of 3.
- Stitch the blocks into rows. Join the rows.
- Stitch the 7/8" x 8" gold plaid strips to opposite sides of the quilt.
- Stitch the 7/8" x 8 3/4" gold plaid strips to the remaining sides of the quilt.
- Stitch two 2 1/4" x 8 3/4" green plaid strips to opposite sides of the quilt.
- Stitch a 2 1/4" red print square to each end of the remaining 2 1/4" x 8 3/4" green plaid strips to make pieced border strips.

- Stitch the pieced border strips to the remaining sides of the quilt.
- Finish the quilt according to the *General Directions*, using the 1 1/4" x 18" green plaid strips for the binding.

Everyone loves Star quilts. Wouldn't this delightful version look just perfect in your home? Make it scrappy or choose colors carefully to match your decor. Either way, you'll love **"Mystery Stars."**

Full-Size Appliqué Patterns for Mine Home Is Where Mine Heart Is (The pattern begins on page 4.)
(Additional patterns are on page 30.)

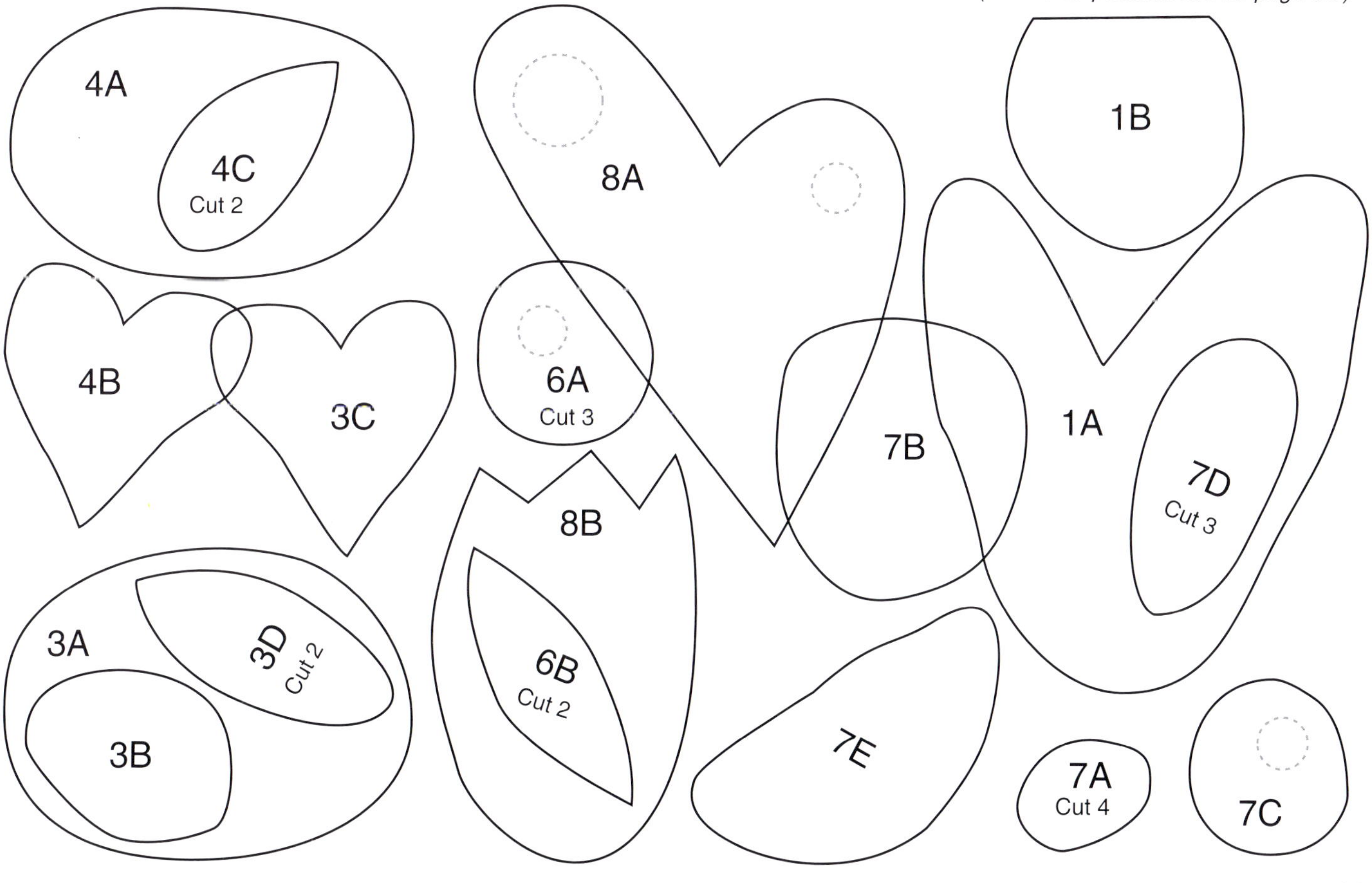

29

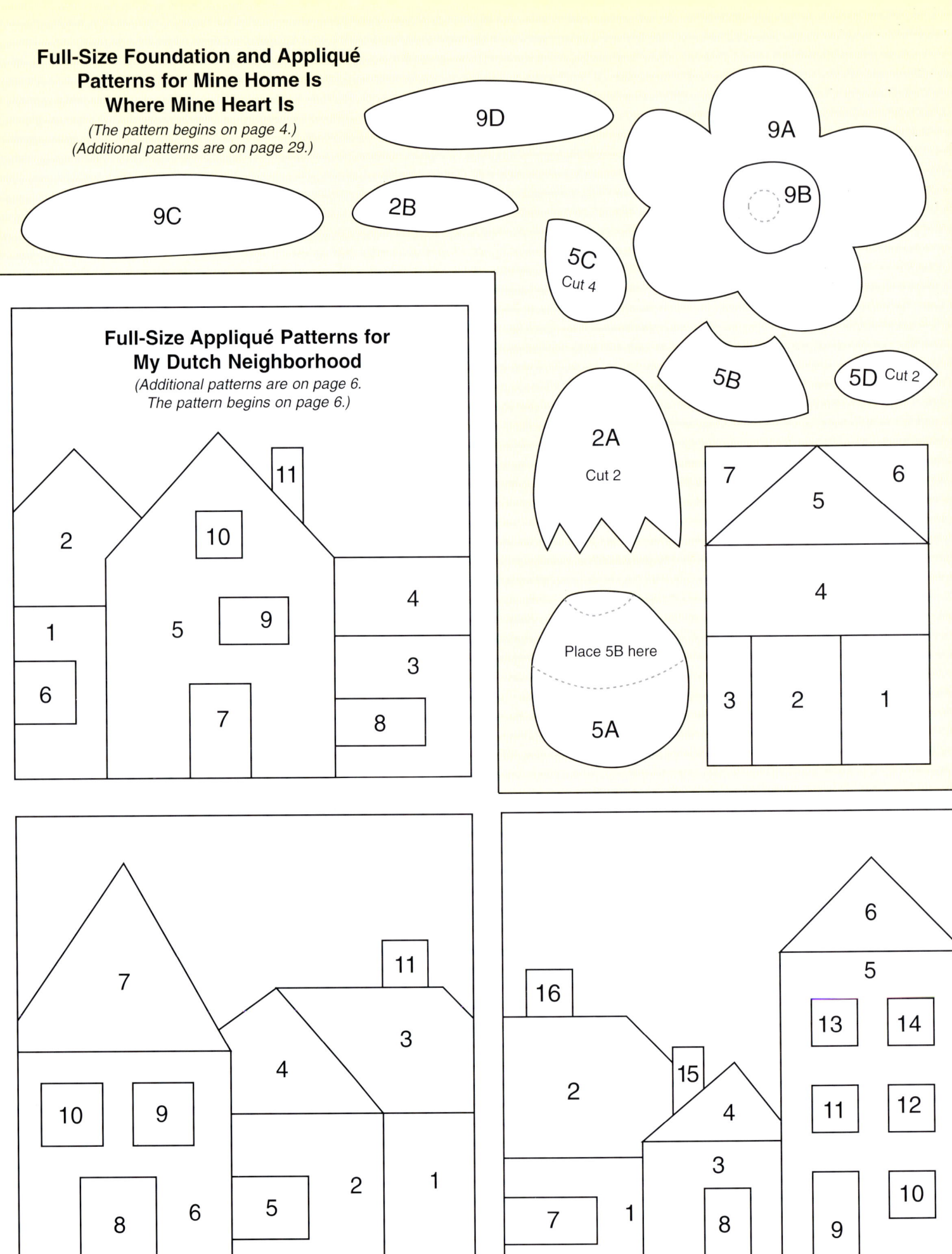

General Directions

About the Patterns

Read through the pattern directions before cutting fabric for the quilt. Pattern directions are presented in step-by-step order.

Fabric

Yardage is based on 44" fabric with a useable width of 42". I recommend using 100% cotton fabrics. Test all of your fabrics to be sure they are colorfast. I suggest washing your fabrics before using them.

Templates

Template patterns are full size and, unless otherwise noted, include a 1/4" seam allowance. The solid line is the cutting line and the broken line is the stitching line. Trace pattern pieces on clear plastic. Use a permanent marker to list the pattern letter and grainline, if one is indicated, on each template. If the instructions call for an R, the template must be reversed before tracing.

Pieced Patterns

For machine piecing, make the template with the seam allowance. Trace around the template on the right side of the fabric. For hand piecing, make the template without the seam allowance. Trace the template on the wrong side of the fabric, flipping all directional (asymmetrical) templates before tracing, and add a 1/4" seam allowance as you cut the fabric pieces out.

Foundation-pieced Patterns

Foundation piecing is a method for making even the smallest blocks with a high degree of accuracy. Foundation patterns are full size and do not include a seam allowance. Cut the foundations out on the outer lines. For each foundation, trace all of the lines and numbers onto paper. You will need one foundation for each block or part of a block as described in the pattern. The inner lines are the stitching lines. The fabric pieces you select do not have to be cut precisely. Be generous when cutting fabric pieces as excess fabric will be trimmed away after sewing. Your goal is to cut a piece that covers the numbered area and extends into surrounding areas after seams are stitched. Generally, fabric pieces should be large enough to extend 1/2" beyond the seamlines on all sides before stitching. For very small sections, or sections without angles, 1/4" may be sufficient. Set the stitch length to 12 stitches per inch.

Place fabric pieces on the unmarked side of the foundation and stitch on the marked side. Center the first piece, right side up, over position 1 on the unmarked side of the foundation. Hold the foundation up to a light to make sure that the raw edges of the fabric extend at least 1/2" beyond the seamline on all sides. Hold this first piece in place with a small dab of glue or a pin, if desired. Place the fabric for position 2 on the first piece, right sides together. Turn the foundation over and sew on the line between 1 and 2, extending the stitching past the beginning and end of the line by a few stitches on both ends. Trim the seam allowance to 1/8". Fold the position 2 piece back, right side up, and press. Continue adding pieces to the foundation in the same manner until all positions are covered and the block is complete. Trim the fabric 1/4" beyond the edges of each foundation.

To avoid disturbing the stitches, do not remove the paper until the blocks have been stitched together and the last border has been added, unless instructed to remove them sooner in the pattern. The pieces will be perforated from the stitching and can be gently pulled free. Use tweezers to carefully remove small sections of the paper, if necessary.

Marking Fabric

Always test marking tools for removability. I suggest using silver or white marking tools for dark fabrics and fine line pencils for light fabrics. Always use a sharp pencil and a light touch. Lay a piece of fine-grained sandpaper under the fabric to keep it from slipping while you mark it, if desired.

Appliqué Patterns

A seam allowance is not included on appliqué patterns. The solid line is the sewing line. Make a template and lightly trace around it on the right side of the fabric. For needleturn appliqué, add a 1/8" to 3/16" turn-under allowance when cutting the fabric pieces out. Clip inside curves almost to the pencil line so they will turn under smoothly as you stitch. Do not add a turn-under allowance if you are using fusible appliqué methods.

Needleturn Appliqué

Pin an appliqué piece in position on the background fabric. Using thread to match the appliqué piece, thread a needle with a 15" to 18" length and knot one end. Turn under the allowance on the appliqué piece, and bring the needle from the wrong side of the background fabric up through the fold on the marked line of the appliqué piece. Push the needle through the background fabric, catching a few threads, and come back up through the background fabric and the appliqué piece on the marked line close to the first stitch. Use the point of the needle to turn under and smooth the allowance, and make another stitch in the same way. Continue needleturning and stitching until the piece is completely sewn to the background fabric. To reduce bulk, do not turn under the allowance or stitch where one appliqué piece will be overlapped by another.

Hand Piecing

Use a thin, short needle (sharp) to ensure a flat seam. Sew only on the marked sewing line using small, even stitches.

Machine Sewing

To make a stitching guide: Cut a length of masking tape or moleskin foot pad about 1/4" x 2". Place a clear plastic ruler under the presser foot to the left of the needle. Slowly slide the ruler to the right until the needle is aligned with the 1/4" mark on the ruler. Lower the presser foot to hold the ruler in place. Carefully adhere the moleskin on the throat plate along the right edge of the ruler. Feed fabric under the needle, touching this guide.

Set the stitch length to 12 stitches per inch. Stitch pieces together from edge to edge unless directed to do otherwise in the pattern. When directions call for you to start or stop stitching 1/4" from edges, as for set-in pieces, backstitch to secure the seam.

Pressing

Press seams toward the darker of the two fabrics unless otherwise noted. Press abutting seams in opposite directions whenever possible. Use a dry iron and press carefully, as little pieces are easy to distort.

Making Bias Strips

Most miniature work requires bias strips of 25" or less. Begin with an 18" fabric square. Lay your clear plastic ruler diagonally across the square, and cut from corner to corner. Cut a bias strip the width you require, measuring from the diagonal cut. This strip will be 25". Additional diagonal cuts will decrease in length. Cut as many strips as are required for your pattern.

Mitering Corners

For mitered borders, the pattern allows extra length on each border strip. Stitch each border to the quilt top, beginning, ending, and backstitching each seamline 1/4" from the edge of the quilt top. After all borders have been attached in this manner, miter one corner at a time. With the quilt top lying right side down, lay one border over the other. Draw a straight line at a 45° angle from the inner corner to the outer corner, as shown.

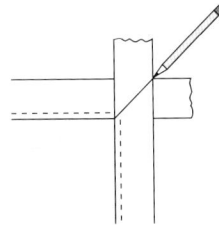

Reverse the positions of the borders and mark another straight line from corner to corner in the same manner.

Place the borders, right sides together. With marked seamlines carefully matched and pinned, stitch from the outer edge to the inner corner, backstitching at the seamline. Open the mitered seam to make sure it lies flat, trim excess fabric, and press.

FINISHING

Marking Quilting Designs

Simple designs can be cut from adhesive-backed shelf paper. They'll stick and re-stick several times. Masking tape can be used to mark grids. Remove the tape when you're not quilting to avoid leaving a sticky residue. Mark lightly with pencils; thick lines that won't go away really stand out on a small quilt.

Batting

Use a thin batting. Layer the quilt sandwich as follows: backing, wrong side up; batting; quilt top, right side up. Baste or pin the layers together.

Quilting

Very small quilts can be lap-quilted without a hoop. Larger ones can be quilted in a hoop or small frame. Use a short, thin needle (between) and small stitches that will be in scale with the little quilt. Thread the needle with a single strand of thread and knot one end. Insert the needle through the quilt top and batting (not the backing) 1/2" away from where you want to begin quilting. Gently pull the thread to pop the knot through the top and bury it in the batting. Quilt as desired.

Binding

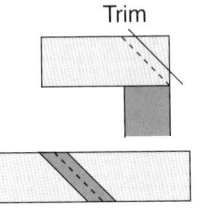

For most straight-edged miniature quilts, a single-fold binding is an attractive, durable, and easy finish. NOTE: *If your quilt has curved or scalloped edges, binding strips must be cut on the bias of the fabric.* Sew the binding strips together with diagonal seams; trim and press the seams open.

Trim one end of the strip at a 45° angle. Press one long edge of the binding strip 1/4" toward the wrong side. Starting with the trimmed end, position the binding strip, right sides together, on the quilt top, aligning the raw edge of the binding with the bottom edge of the quilt top. Leaving approximately 2" of the binding strip free, and beginning at least 3 inches from one corner, stitch the binding to the bottom of the quilt with a 1/4" seam allowance, measuring from the edge of the binding and quilt top.

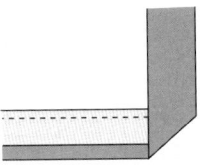

When you reach a corner, stop the stitching line exactly 1/4" from the edge of the quilt top. Backstitch, clip threads, and remove the quilt from the machine. Fold the binding up and away, creating a 45° angle, as shown.

Fold the binding down as shown, and begin stitching at the edge.

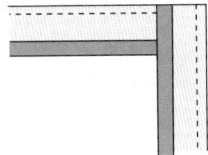

Continue stitching around the quilt to within 2" of the starting point. Lay the binding flat against the quilt, overlapping the beginning end. Open the pressed edge on each end, and fold the end of the binding at a 45° angle against the angle on the beginning end of the binding. Finger press the fold.

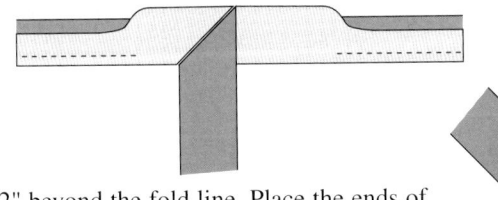

Trim 1/2" beyond the fold line. Place the ends of the binding right sides together, and stitch with a 1/4" seam allowance. Finger press the seam allowance open.

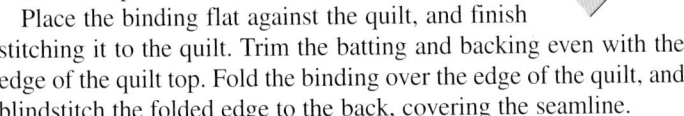

Place the binding flat against the quilt, and finish stitching it to the quilt. Trim the batting and backing even with the edge of the quilt top. Fold the binding over the edge of the quilt, and blindstitch the folded edge to the back, covering the seamline.

Sign Your Quilt

Small quilts are revered by collectors, and the little quilts we make today will be treasured by our families and friends. Using embroidery, cross-stitch, or permanent marker, write your name and other important data like your city, the date the quilt was completed, and for whom the quilt was made on a label, and stitch it to the quilt. Someone will be glad you did!